WHAT'S LURKING IN THIS HOUSE?

In This Kitchen

Nancy Harris

www.raintreepublishers.co.uk
Visit our website to find out
more information about
Raintree books.

To order:
☎ Phone 0845 6044371
📄 Fax +44 (0) 1865 312263
💻 Email myorders@raintreepublishers.co.uk

Customers from outside the UK please telephone +44 1865 312262

Raintree is an imprint of Capstone Global Library Limited,
a company incorporated in England and Wales having its
registered office at 7 Pilgrim Street, London, EC4V 6LB
– Registered company number: 6695582

Text © Capstone Global Library Limited 2010
First published in hardback in 2010
First published in paperback in 2011
The moral rights of the proprietor have been asserted.

Edited by Rebecca Rissman, Nancy Dickmann,
 and Sian Smith
Designed by Joanna Hinton-Malivoire
Original illustrations © Capstone Global Library Ltd., 2010
Illustrated by Kevin Rechin
Picture research by Tracy Cummins
Originated by Capstone Global Library Ltd
Printed and bound in China by Leo Paper
 Products Ltd

ISBN 978 140621318 8 (hardback)
14 13 12 11 10
10 9 8 7 6 5 4 3 2 1

ISBN 978 140621324 9 (paperback)
14 13 12 11 10
10 9 8 7 6 5 4 3 2 1

British Library Cataloguing in Publication Data
Harris, Nancy.
 What's lurking in this house?.
 In this kitchen.
 1. Household pests--Juvenile literature. 2. Microbial
 ecology--Juvenile literature. 3. Kitchens--Juvenile
 literature.
 I. Title
 579.1'7-dc22

Acknowledgements
The author and publisher are grateful to the following for
permission to reproduce copyright material: Alamy p.**17**
(© Maximilian Weinzierl); Dwight Kuhn Photography p.**9**
(© Dwight Kuhn); Getty Images p.**12** (Jim Doberman);
Photo Researchers, Inc. pp.**7** (© Nigel Cattlin), **21** (©
Gusto), **23 bottom** (© Scimat), **25** (© Eye of Science),
27 bottom (© Cordelia Molloy); Photolibrary pp.**6**
(Imagesource), **28** (Digital Vision); Photoshot p.**11**
(Bruce Cocleman/Edward Snow); Shutterstock pp.**10**
(© PetrP), **13** (© Ronald van der Beek), **15 bottom** (©
Johanna Goodyear), **15 top** (© Studiotouch), **23 top**
(© Bochkarev Photography), **24** (© karovka), **27 top** (©
Gertjan Hooijer), **29 fly** (© Liew Weng Keong), **29 roach**
(© Connie Wade); Visuals Unlimited, Inc. pp.**19** (© Nigel
Cattlin), **20** (© Dr. James L. Castner).
Cover photograph of an American cockroach reproduced
with permission of FLPA (© Nigel Cattlin).

Every effort has been made to contact copyright holders
of any material reproduced in this book. Any omissions
will be rectified in subsequent printings if notice is given
to the publisher.

Some words are shown in bold, **like this**. You can find
out what they mean by looking in the glossary.

Contents

Is something lurking in this house?

A house is a place where you eat, sleep, work, and play. The kitchen is where food is kept. Have you ever thought about what might be living there with the food?

FUN FACT

You might think bathrooms are bad, but sometimes the kitchen is the dirtiest room in the house!

5

Dinner time!

You are helping to make dinner. You go to a cupboard to get some rice. What you find lurking there is more than you expected!

Rice weevils are tiny creatures. You might find them living in rice, cereals, and other foods.

grain of rice

rice weevil

Who is eating your food?

Inside a cereal box you see mealworms munching away. You cannot miss them. They are golden brown. You look in the cupboard. Mealworms are also in the flour and macaroni.

mealworm

Some mealworms are over two centimetres long! That's about the same length as a paperclip.

Mealworms are not worms. They are insects. As they grow up they change, or **metamorphose**, into beetles. They eat all day and at night.

FUN FACT

A mealworm can lose, or **shed**, its skin up to 20 times before becoming an adult.

skin

This black mealworm beetle is eating bread that has been left out.

Eating mealworms

Birds and fish like to eat mealworms. So do some people. They say mealworms are very tasty. What do you think? Would a mealworm snack be a good idea?

FUN FACT

Mealworms are low in fat and can be a good source of food.

Feasting on your fruit!

Fruit flies are very small insects. You might see them swarming around your fruit bowl. They feast on fruit and vegetables that have been left out.

This shows a fruit fly up close.

actual size
of a fruit fly

Crawling cockroaches

Another insect crawling in the kitchen could be a cockroach. They like to live in dark places, such as under a fridge. They also like warm and **moist**, or damp, places.

cockroach

FUN FACT

A cockroach can live without its head for a week. It dies of thirst after a week because it can't drink water without a mouth!

In kitchens there are lots of dark places for cockroaches to hide.

Cockroaches have oval shaped bodies. They have **antennae** and six legs. Some have wings. Cockroaches are hard to get rid of.

FUN FACT
Most cockroaches have at least 18 knees!

antennae

knees

wings

Cockroaches crawl around on your kitchen worktops. They move around in your food and on your dishes. As they crawl they may carry **germs** around your kitchen. Germs are very small living things that can make you ill.

cockroach

Putting lids on your bottles will help keep out cockroaches and germs!

tomato sauce

FUN FACT

Cockroaches can climb walls because they have little claws on their feet.

Watch out for germs!

Your kitchen is full of **germs**. Many germs are so small that you can only see them with a **microscope.** There are many types of germs.

Many germs can live in your kitchen sink.

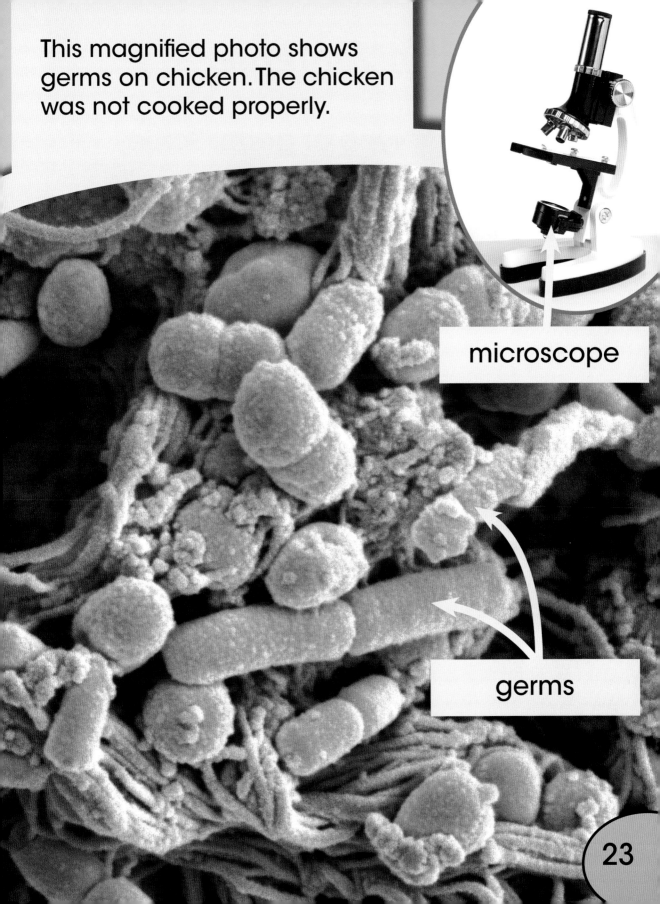

This magnified photo shows germs on chicken. The chicken was not cooked properly.

microscope

germs

Harmful bacteria

Bacteria is a type of **germ**. Some bacteria in your kitchen can make you ill. Bacteria likes to eat dead pieces of plants and animals.

FUN FACT

Millions of bacteria can often be found on one kitchen sponge!

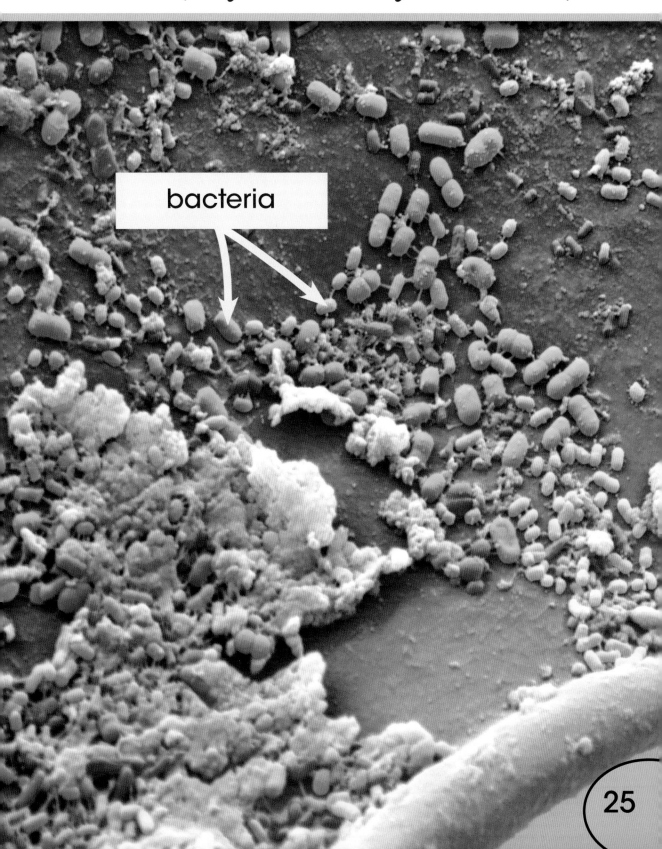

A kitchen sponge seen through a microscope.

bacteria

Yuk! Mould

Mould is a small living thing. It can grow on food. Mould can grow on bread and cheese. It can be blue, white, or black. Look at food before you eat it. Mould can make you ill.

mould

mould

mould

27

Keeping it clean

It is important to keep the kitchen clean. Putting dishes and sponges in a dishwasher can help kill **germs**. Worktops can be washed with special soap. Cleaning up food scraps will help to keep away creatures. It will also help keep away **bacteria** and mould.

Fun facts

Cockroaches can recognise each other by smell. Imagine if we could do that!

Cockroaches can swim. They can hold their breath for up to 40 minutes.

Cockroaches have white blood.

Mealworms will eat the bodies of dead mice or rats. They eat the bodies if they are old and dry.

Sadly for them, adult fruit flies only live for about 8 to 10 days.

Glossary

antennae pair of feelers attached to the head of an insect

bacteria tiny living things. Bacteria are a type of germ.

germs tiny living things that can make you ill if they get inside your body

metamorphose to change into something else

microscope instrument used to see very small things, such as germs

moist wet or damp

shed to take off and get rid of something

Find out more

Books

Bug Books: Cockroach, Karen Hartley, Chris Macro, and Phillip Taylor (Heinemann Library, 2nd Edition, 2006)

Germs, Ross Collins (Bloomsbury Publishing, 2005)

Watch it Grow: Mealworms, Martha E.H. Rustad (Capstone Press, 2009)

Where to Find Minibeasts: Minibeasts in the Home, Sarah Ridley (Smart Apple Media, 2009)

Find out

Which creature uses its mouth to both smell and taste?

Websites

http://www.pestworldforkids.org/flies.html
Learn about flies on this website and read the fact file on fruit flies.

http://www.mikki.net/mealworms.htm
This website has information on mealworms and on the life cycle of a mealworm.

http://yucky.discovery.com/flash/roaches/
Find out about a day in the life of a cockroach and learn some amazing cockroach facts on this website.

Index

PILLGWENLLY
23-07-18